The Quakers of Mosedale

The First Publishers of Truth

In the year 1653 George Fox came to Mosedale, a tiny hamlet in the parish of Caldbeck, on the north-eastern flank of Skiddaw, where the river Caldew tumbles down the lovely valley between Carrock Fell and Bowscale and the most familiar sound is the liquid call of the curlew. He held a meeting at the house of John Slee in Mungrisdale, two miles to the south and with him were Robert Widders (or Withers), Edward Burrough and John Blaykling, all men who became well known in the north and throughout England as valiant upholders of the Truth and who, like George Fox, were imprisoned for their beliefs. Robert Widders was described by Fox as a 'thunderinge man against hypocrisy and deceite and hy rotteness of ye priests'. Edward Burrough in the short space of ten years rose to take a foremost place among Friends; he laboured incessantly both by word and pen and died in the abomination of Newgate gaol. John Blaykling was a Yorkshireman, a farmer from Draw-well near Sedburgh and he and others of his family gave valuable service to the Society.

These three men and the inspiration of George Fox drew together the first meeting of Friends of Mosedale, to which came Thomas Mark, John Todhunter, William Greenhow, Hugh Peacock and several others.[1] It may seem strange to us now that in such a remote valley among the Cumberland hills men and women were prepared to make long journeys on foot and on horseback, along roads which were no more than rough cart tracks, to hear the word of God preached by strangers, but in many ways the north-western countries were a fertile breeding ground for Quakerism. The history of the Church of England in its isolated country parishes was not inspiring; it was reported of Bromfield,

---

[1] Penney (Norman) ed. *First Publishers of Truth*, 1907, p.51.

for example, that for forty seven years no vicar had resided in the parish.[2] The more fortunate clergy rode to hounds and enjoyed a life of ease and pleasure, but at the other end of the scale were the poor curates, often no better off than the poorest of their parishioners and whose infrequent ministrations were all that stood between the people and heathenism. During the Cromwellian period a total of thirty one clergy in the diocese of Carlisle and deaconries of Coupland and Kendale were ejected from their livings[3] and control of the parishes was divided between various sects, especially Independants and Presbyterians. Presbyterianism had a strong hold on the north of Cumberland, due to the numbers of Scots who had come over the border and who brought their own religion to their new homes. There was also a third Lutheran element. The story of mining in its various forms runs through the history of Cumbria; many of the early mining engineers were German in origin and between 1564, when Thomas Thurland and Daniel Hoechstetter were authorised to seek for gold, and 1567 there was a steady influx of foreign workers into the Lake counties. By 1567 no less than fourteen of them had married English girls and settled in England.[4] So out of these three elements, dissatisfaction with the administration of the Church of England, the influence of Presbyterianism and the small Lutheran element there grew up in the Lake District groups of Seekers who in their spiritual starvation sought a personal way to God and to these people the message of George Fox was like a great light shining in their darkness. It was only in the previous year, 1652, that Fox, a man not yet twenty eight years old, had held his great meeting on Firbank Fell in Lancashire, when the people came in their hundreds to this creative moment in the history of Quakerism. So convinced were the men of Mosedale of the Truth he preached that many 'did suffere much for it since by impriseinment and spoiling of Goods

[2] Bouch (C.M.L.) and Jones (G.P.) *Short Economic and Social History of the Lake Counties* 1500-1830. Manchester University Press, 1962.
[3] Bouch (C.M.L.) *Prelates and People of the Lake Counties: history of the diocese of Carlisle.* Kendal: Titus Wilson, 1948, p. 265.
[4] Bouch and Jones, *op. cit.*, p. 120.

for non payment of tythes. Jno Sowerby suffered fifteen years Impriseinment and upwards, John Todhunter eight years and upwards, William Greenhow six and upwards, all which Cruell sufering they did Chearfully undergo. Some of which have finished this mortall rase, others remaining held their Integrity'.[5] Richard Atkinson, who was also an early member of the meeting, was disowned and banished from his father's house, until later on George Fox advised him to return to his father; he did go back and found that his father's heart had softened towards him and he 'tooke him in, and afterwards Loved him above ye rest of his children'.[6]

John Slee, at whose house the first meeting of Mosedale Friends was held, was a member of an old Cumberland family and lived at Grisedale How in the barony of Greystoke. After his convincement he became one of the Valiant Sixty, a company of men and women mainly from the north-west of England who started their service in the cause of Truth between the years 1652 and 1654.[7] We catch glimpses of this Friend on his journeys up and down the country and his name appears several times in the accounts of the general stock managed from Swarthmoor, a centre of Quaker activity and the home of Margaret Fell, who some years after the death of her husband Judge Fell became the wife of George Fox.

The Settlement of Mosedale Meeting

After the meeting at John Slee's house in 1653 a meeting was settled at Mosedale; the number of early Friends who comprised this meeting is not at present known, but from records in the Library at Friends House in London it appears that they met for worship in one another's houses and endured persecution for their beliefs. In the year 1660 goods to a total value of about £515 were taken from them for tithes

[5] Penney, *op.. cit.*, p. 51.
[6] *Ibid.*, p. 51.
[7] Taylor (Ernest E.) *The Valiant Sixty*. London: Bannisdale, rev. edn., 1951, p.9.

worth only £156 and between the years 1681 and 1690 the value of barley, sheep and other goods in kind taken from them amounted to over £2,000. The rector of Caldbeck between the years 1664-1700 was Arthur Savage and he was assiduous in his persecution of the Quakers, who refused to pay tithes and church rents for the support of what they termed a 'hireling ministry'. The story of the Bewleys, a notable Cumberland family some of whose members went to Ireland, where they are still active supporters of the Society, does not really belong to the chronicle of Mosedale; George Bewley represented Mosedale at county meetings in the seventeenth century[8] but the family later worshipped with Friends at Woodhall and Gillfoot. However, the case of Thomas Bewley of Haltcliffe Hall is worth quoting as an example of the lengths to which Arthur Savage was prepared to go:

Anno 1673. Thomas Bewley of Hatcliffe Hall, aged about 78, was prosecuted by Arthur Savage, priest, for £3 prescription money, and had taken from him his feather bed, bed clothes, and a cupboard worth £5. The hardship of the poor old man's case so affected the neighbourhood with compassion, that when the bayliff exposed these goods to sale, nobody would buy them at any rate; whereupon the priest sued the bayliff, and made him pay both his demand and his costs.

Anno 1674. On the 1st of November, this year, the same priest again prosecuted the said Thomas Bewley for tithe of wool, lambs &c, and, notwithstanding his very great age, sent him to prison.[9] These early Quakers were not for the most part wealthy men; in Cumberland they were yeomen or husbandmen and among the list of occupations given for the Valiant Sixty only one man is described as a gentleman.[10] Their comparative poverty at this period is borne out by an examination of Wills in the Record Office at Carlisle. Christopher Todhunter of Bowscale, who died in 1712, left legacies

[8] Cumberland QM minutes, 29th January 1689.
[9] Besse (Joseph) *Collection of the Sufferings of the People called Quakers*, 1753, vol. 1, p. 132.
[10] Taylor, *op. cit.*, pp. 40-1.

of 1/- to his brother Hugh, 6d to each of his brother's children and £8 to each of his three daughters; Elizabeth Todhunter of Mungrisdale, who could not read or write, owned worldly goods to the value of only £7 10s.0d. and her total estate was only £22; George Bewley of Woodhall, who died in 1664 and at whose house George Fox stayed, left about £65, but his household goods included some pewter, whereas the very poor would use wooden implements, and he was also owed £100 so he may have been a banker in a small way. It is interesting to make a comparison with his descendant Thomas Bewley, who died in 1747, nearly a hundred years later, leaving goods to the value of £222 and money owing to him of over £2,000. The minutes of Caldbeck Monthly Meeting, of which Mosedale was part, bear out the poverty of Friends in Mosedale and often contain provision for small sums for their relief.

The houses in which these early Quakers lived were typical of the period. They were built of stone, with a flagged passage running from the front to the back of the house. On one side of this passage were the byre and stables and on the other side were the main rooms, consisting of a kitchen or house place, with a parlour or bower opening off it. The only fireplace was in the kitchen, a substantial structure built of stone, where all the cooking was done and from which the whole house was warmed. A wealthy farmer would add more rooms as he required them and each room had a loft over it, to which at first access was by a rough ladder, although at about this time staircases were beginning to be built in separate annexes attached to the main building, and the lofts converted into bedrooms. Thomas Bewley's house at Woodhall had five rooms and a staircase and was therefore quite substantial.

The Building of the Meeting House

For the first hundred and fifty years of its existence the story of Mosedale is that of the Quaker families who made up the meeting, many of whom were descendants of the first Friends who went to George

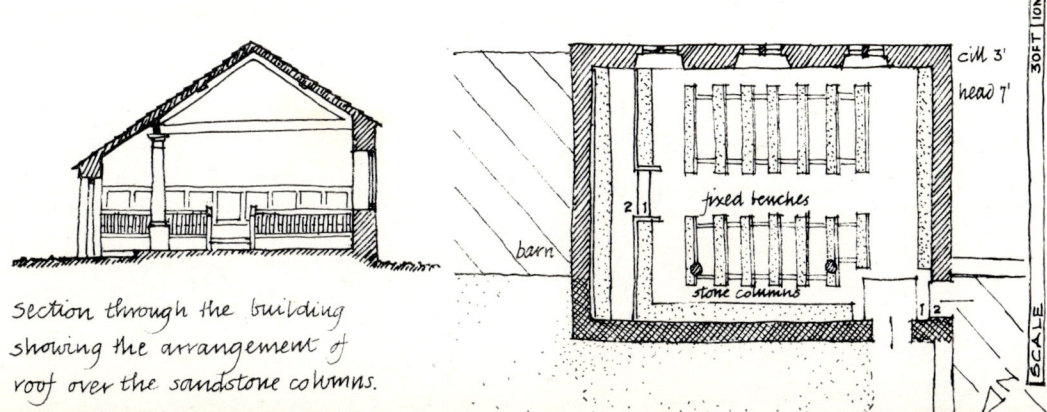

cill 3'
head 7'

fixed benches

stone columns

barn

2 1

1 2

SCALE 30FT 10M

N

Section through the building
showing the arrangement of
roof over the sandstone columns.

7

Fox's meeting in 1653. It is probable that it was not until about the end of the seventeenth century that they were sufficiently well established to build a meeting house, but the origin of the meeting house is obscure. It is said that 'Soon after [1653] a Meeting was settled and yet remains called Mosedale Meeting: Tho. Mark, Jno Sowerby, Jno Greenhow, Hugh Peacock and several others . . . and there is an increase this year [?] for that Meeting is enlarged and they have builded a Meeting House at Mosedale . . . and the children come . . . Jno Sowerby 15yrs., John Todhunter 8 yrs., William Greenhow 6 yrs., also Richard Atkinson brought by his father'.[11] According to the date over the door the meeting house was completed in 1702, but it was not then the property of Friends. There is no record in the minutes of Cumberland Quarter Sessions for the issue of a licence for it, only on 15th July 1702 it is 'ordered that the house of George Peacock in Mosedale be recorded for the publick worship of the people called Quakers'.[12] So it appears that for some years at any rate the meeting house was the private property of George Peacock and later of his son or nephew Hugh Peacock and was in fact part of his house and land. Almost opposite to the meeting house there is a building which was used during the last century for storing oats, but which may at one time have been a dwelling house. Above the bricked up doorway is a stone with the initials H H P carved upon it, with the date 1735; it was the common practice for a man to inscribe the initials of himself and his wife above the doorway of their home and it is possible that this house belonged to Hugh Peacock and that he married about the year 1735. The farm house on the other side of the road, above the meeting house, may have belonged to George Peacock.

The first and indeed the only existing deed relating to the meeting house is an indenture drawn up

[11] Ferguson (Richard S.) *Early Cumberland and Westmorland Friends: a series of biographical sketches of early members of the Society of Friends in those counties.* London: F. Bowyer Kitto, 1871. Quoted in *A Quaker Saga* by Jane W. T. Brey. Philadelphia: Dorrance & Co., 1967, p. 26.
[12] Minutes of Cumberland Quarter Sessions, 15th July 1702, (Cumbria Record Office, Carlisle. Q/6/1).

in 1739, in which Hugh Peacock transferred the ownership of the meeting house, small school house, burial ground and a yard to George Priestman, Daniel Wilson, John Barn, John Slee, John Mark, Christopher Todhunter and George Mark as trustees for 'the people called Quakers'. There are several interesting points about this deed. Its wording suggests that although for many years the meeting house remained in the possession of George and Hugh Peacock the actual building was carried out by Friends; the deed describes 'one burying place as itt is walled about one meeting house and a little house both erected upon his [Hugh Peacock's] ground in Mosedale one yard walled about all done att the proper costs and charges of the people called Quakers as also four yards on the south side of the said houses'. The reference to the little house being used as a school is also interesting. There is no other record of the establishment of a school in Mosedale and the number of pupils can only have been very small; the room is tiny and now houses the meeting house cloakrooms. This little room was also intended to be used for the women's preparative meeting and very cramped and uncomfortable it must have been. The original meeting house, a long low building like a stable, may have been converted from an open fronted barn, the roof of which would normally in the north of the county have been supported by substantial wooden pillars. The two red sandstone pillars which are such a feature of the present building are unusual; it is possible that they are contemporary with the original structure, but they may have replaced wooden pillars during the extensive repairs and reconstruction which took place in 1884. There are indications in the stone work that the side of the meeting house facing the road has been extended by about five feet and the position of the pillars is in line with the original frontage; the roof has also at some time been raised and the line of the original roof can clearly be seen in the plastering over the gallery. Other features which date from the seventeenth century are probably the stone flagged floor, the oak steps leading up to the gallery and the uninviting oak benches, which were originally backless. Eighteenth-century meetings were usually very long, lasting three to four hours, and these benches must have been a sad trial to the younger members of the meeting. Why Friends settled their meeting at Mosedale rather than at Mungrisdale can only be a matter for speculation, but it is probable that Mosedale provided a more convenient meeting place for Friends from the scattered hamlets and farmsteads round about. The two villages also differed in character. In 1704 there were in Mungrisdale only one dwelling house and twenty two tenements, whereas there were in Mosedale seven houses and four in the neighbouring hamlet of Swinside, further up the Caldew valley.[13]

The meeting house was of course built primarily as a place where Friends could meet together to practise their own form of the silent worship of God, but it was also used for burials and marriages. There is a record in the Caldbeck parish register of a marriage in Mosedale meeting house in 1704 and of a burial in 1703, but authentic records of the use of the meeting house for these purposes do not begin until 1714 with the burial of Bridgett Bristo and the marriage in 1715/16 of Joseph Bristo of Swinside to Mary Peet.[14] The Bristos were an early Quaker family who appear to have died out in the second generation; there is only one entry for them in the local records kept by Caldbeck Monthly Meeting and now lodged at the Public Record Office. The Peets reappeared in Mosedale in the early nineteenth century, but nothing is known of their early history. A study of the registers in the Library at Friends House shows how the original families continued to uphold Quakerism in this remote and lonely valley, not always to the liking of the clergy of the Established Church, one of whom wrote in 1747 that Caldbeck, to which Mosedale Meeting belonged, was 'greatly overrun, as all these mountains

[13] Nicholson (William) *Miscellany Accounts of the Diocese of Carlisle.* London, 1877, p. 225
[14] Cumberland and Northumberland QM Marriages and Burial Digests (Friends House Library, London).

are, with Quakers, who have three meeting houses in this parish. They are fewer than they were when I first came. I am thankful they are not increased'. [15] The registers at Friends House also throw an interesting light on the families who appear to have been the backbone of the meeting in Mosedale up to the year 1837. All through the marriage records the names of the original Friends recur; Peacock, Mark, Todhunter and Slee. The Slees were a Mungrisdale family who flourished in the century between 1650 and 1750 and eighteen children are recorded as having been born to various members during this period; Peacocks, but not Todhunters, appear in the birth records, but the Marks, an old Cumberland family, dominated Mosedale Meeting throughout the eighteenth and early nineteenth centuries. They largely disappeared during the nineteenth century, to be replaced by the Peacocks and the Peets, and probably left the Society or sought a livelihood elsewhere. Some of the old Quaker names still survive in the district around Mosedale and many of the villagers and neighbouring farmers have Quaker ancestors; there are still Todhunters to be found, and Wilsons, but Marks and Peacocks have disappeared beyond the memory of the oldest inhabitants of the village.

Friends in the Eighteenth and Nineteenth Centuries

Several notable Friends travelling in the ministry visited Mosedale during the eighteenth century, but only the briefest reference to it appears in their journals and it is not possible to form an impression of what is was like nor how large it was. It was not increased by convincement and inevitably the younger members of the Quaker families did not always remain faithful to the beliefs and principles of their fathers. By 1770 it was becoming increasingly difficult to find a representative to send to Caldbeck Monthly Meeting; sometimes no one went, sometimes only one man and it made no difference whether

[15] Mounsey—Heysham MSS. Miscellany Accounts of the Diocese 1703-4, with additional notes by Archdeacon Waugh, 1747, p. 70 (Cumbria Record Office, Carlisle).

it was winter or summer. When a representative was sent it was usually a member of the Marks family.

In 1831 Caldbeck Monthly Meeting, which was itself in a very low state, was dissolved and united with Carlisle Monthly Meeting, so that henceforward the welfare of the small company of Quakers in Mosedale became the concern of Carlisle Friends. As early as 1815 the state of their meeting had been a matter of concern to Caldbeck Friends, but the decline in their numbers was not a local phenomenon; it was a reflection of the state of the Society as a whole. The years from the turn of the century onwards were difficult for the Quaker movement. The full story is a very long one, but the main reasons for the disquiet felt by the leaders of the Society lay in the Evangelical revival, which caused many Friends to turn to the Church of England or other religious denominations which practised the rites of baptism and the Lord's Supper; the growing impatience of young Friends with the marriage regulations, under which until 1859 it was impossible to marry a non-Friend at meeting, so that disownment for marriage before a priest was the inevitable outcome; and the fact that over the years Quakers, because of their integrity in business matters, had in many cases become wealthy and some at least turned to Unitarianism, finding their spiritual home in the form of religious worship practised by their social equals.

In spite of the dissolution of Caldbeck Monthly Meeting, in 1850 weekday meetings were still being held at Mosedale and at the Quaker census of church attendance taken in 1851 Mosedale Friends accounted for six of the total number of one hundred and seventy eight attendances at morning and afternoon Friends' meetings in the Carlisle area;[16] in 1852 a group of Friends from Carlisle was appointed to sit with the faithful remnant at Mosedale as and when they could. But by 1864 Mosedale no longer appeared in the Book of Meetings as a place of regular worship, although the meeting house

[16] Quaker census of attendance, 1851-1941 (Friends House Library, London).

continued to be used from time to time.

There is a gap in the records from 1854 to 1877, but about 1880 the meeting, of which there were only a handful of members left, enjoyed a resurgence for which there is at present no certain explanation. In 1884 Carlisle Monthly Meeting felt it worth while to embark on the extensive repairs and alterations which have given the meeting house substantially the appearance it presents today. The roof may have been raised at this time, the windows on the south side enlarged; the gallery was panelled in pine and backs were added to the uncomfortable benches; the little room whose use has never been clearly determined was turned into a primitive cloakroom. The whole restoration was completed at a cost of about £50; a breakdown of the costs shows no trace of the sandstone pillars having been added at this time, but they may have been given to the meeting. In September 1884 Carlisle Monthly Meeting decided to let Mosedale to the Methodists at an annual rental of £1 for seven years, the whole sum being payable in advance, but this decision was rescinded in the following month and the administration of the meeting house was left in the hands of John Strong of Deerrudding, to grant or refuse its use on particular days according as it might be required by Friends.

It is possible that the activities of the Home Mission Committee may have influenced this decision. This Committee was set up by London Friends in November 1881 after a conference convened by the Friends' First-day School Association and the committee of the Bedford Institute. Its purpose was to help in the re-opening and re-establishment of closed or decaying meetings and it functioned through a committee composed largely of people who were prepared to give their time and money to the work, or who could work to support themselves during their missionary activity. It fostered work in Sunday Schools, in the study of the Bible and in the Adult School movement and did much practical charitable work in addition always to the task of propagating the beliefs and principles of the Society. In 1885

Frederick Sessions spent a week in Mosedale at the invitation of the Quarterly Meeting[17] and as a result of his activity Bible classes were started on Sundays. There is also a note in the minutes of Cumberland Quarterly Meeting for 24th September 1885 that meetings for worship were held at Mosedale on alternate Sundays, but there is no indication as to when this practice started or how long it continued.

In 1891 Howard Nicholson was liberated for religious service in Cumberland and visited Mosedale in October, but he has left no description of the conditions he found there. However, it appears that the visits of these ministering Friends had stimulated interest in the Quaker movement in Mosedale and although by 1894 there were only four members of the Society left in the village and the surrounding countryside, there was a very large number of attenders, far more than for any of the meetings making up Carlisle Monthly Meeting, or even for Carlisle itself. In 1894 there were twenty three attenders and the figure continued at about or slightly below this level until 1901, when it abruptly ceased. The census returns for 1891 give the total population of the village as fifty nine[18] and although this figure probably relates only to the village itself and does not include outlying farms, some of which were still in Quaker hands, it is difficult to determine where these attenders came from or why they left so abruptly. Some may have come from Mungrisdale; it is also possible that the meetings were more in the nature of revivalist Bible services than Quaker meetings for worship and that they attracted people inspired by the Wesleyan Home Missions which were being held at that time throughout Cumberland.[19] But it is curious that the attendance should have ceased so suddenly, especially with the influx into the village in 1901 of the men re-opening Carrock mine at the head of the Caldew valley above Mosedale.

[17] Report of Home Mission Committee in *London YM Proceedings*, 1886, p. 22.
[18] 1891 Census Returns (Cumbria Record Office, Carlisle).
[19] *Mid Cumberland and North Westmorland Herald*, 9th February 1895.

The Quiet Years

After its brief revival Mosedale Meeting house settled back to slumber among the quiet hills. John Strong, into whose hands it had been given, reported in 1907 that meetings for worship were still held on Sundays, with a prospect of a week-day meeting, but there were at that time only two members of the Society remaining in the Mosedale area. The meeting house was also used as a reading room for the men working at the Carrock mine and for occasional prayer meetings, but by 1913 Carlisle Friends felt that the time had come for the meeting to be formally 'laid down', and for Mosedale Friends to become members of Carlisle Particular Meeting. This was done in April 1913 and it seemed that Mosedale's long history as a place of Quaker worship and a centre of Quaker activity was drawing to a close.[20]

But Quakerism in Mosedale is a living force which will not be denied. On 30th November 1914 John Strong wrote to the monthly meeting that: 'With regard to Mosedale, meetings are held regularly once a month by John Sinclair and my eldest daughter is looking forward to holding Friends' Meetings in the spring'.[21] In 1915 George Prior of Cockermouth held a meeting at Mosedale which was largely attended both by Friends and people from the surrounding countryside. George Prior had travelled extensively in the service of the ministry in Scotland and Ireland; he was a gentle, quiet man with a liking for poetry and often quoted Whittier to his appreciative audiences. He loved children and young people and it would be pleasant to think that he re-kindled the light of Quakerism in the hearts of the young people of Mosedale. But unfortunately, although Carlisle Friends felt his visit to be timely and helpful and were encouraged to a renewed concern for the outlying meetings in their care, they were

[20] Minutes of Carlisle MM, 2nd March 1913 and 6th April 1913; confirmed by minute of Cumberland QM 26th March 1913.
[21] Extract from a letter from John Strong of Deerrudding in minutes of Carlisle United Preparative and Monthly Meeting, 1914.

not able to build on the interest which his visit had aroused. After John Strong's death in 1917 the meeting house appears mainly to have been used for many years as a chapel by the Methodists, whose rousing services are still remembered by older people in the village, and by the Church of England for a service once a month and at Harvest Festival times. The monthly services were poorly attended, but the Harvest Festivals were occasions of general thanksgiving and attracted large congregations. During all this period the cleaning and caretaking of the 'Quaker chapel' was undertaken by several of the residents of Mosedale. In 1976 they still remembered the more major tasks of whitewashing, floor washing and stove lighting.

The building of course still belonged to Friends. It had to be insured and maintained even to be available for its limited use as a chapel and for the occasional use of organisations like the Mosedale branch of the National Amalgamated Union of Labour, who, in periods when the Carrock mine was in operation, used it fortnightly for the transaction of their business. The small library, which had continued to be used and cared for until the meeting was laid down, could not be neglected. But by 1970 it was estimated that £80 would be the minimum cost of the repairs necessary merely to patch up the fabric, make it weatherproof and protect it from the fate of dereliction which had overtaken so many of the small meeting houses in Cumberland, many of which had been sold out of the Society of Friends.* The Methodist connection with the building had long since ceased, although the Church of England continued to use it until 1972. Various suggestions for its future use were made; young Friends wanted to use it as a meeting place and there was a proposal that it should be adapted as a holiday centre for poor children from the slum areas of large cities. But in spite of its historic associations with early Quakerism, Carlisle and Holm Monthly Meeting felt that both the meeting house and burial

* Keswick (1801), Gillfoot (1922), Whelpo (1923), Kirkbride (1926), Whitehaven (1931) and Sikeside (1951).

ground, last used in 1921, should be sold; they did not want to be responsible for its maintenance and complaints had been received about the neglected state of the meeting house and burial ground.

Restoration

But two members of the monthly meeting had a practical plan for its continued use as a Quaker meeting house. Beryl Hibbs and Coryn Clarke, then Clerk to Carlisle and Holm Monthly Meeting, proposed that they should rent the building from the monthly meeting, restore it and use it not only for Quaker meetings but also as a coffee house for the use of walkers and visitors to the northern fells.

The work to be done to achieve even these limited aims was considerable. Planning permission had to be obtained and this was a lengthy and exasperating business, involving much correspondence. The whole structure had to be made good and then painted; water and electricity had to be laid on, a drainage system constructed, a small kitchen equipped and proper cloakrooms provided. All this work was done by local Friends with a minimum of professional assistance and the help of a six day work camp of international students from Woodbrooke. The capital expenditure involved has been about £1200 and the project was financed initially by a bank loan to Beryl Hibbs and a grant of £500 from the Quaker Meeting Houses Fund; later on Carlisle and Holm Monthly Meeting made a grant of £200 and a further interest free loan of £200 (which has now been repaid), and about £500 has been received in donations from Friends in many parts of the country. The amount of money needed would of course have been very much more than £1200 if Quakers in the area had not done so much of the work themselves and been willing to devote so much of their time and personal resources to it.

After restoration the meeting house celebrated its re-opening on 21st July 1973, when about forty-five people met for worship. In that year the coffee shop opened only for the month of August. From

1974 it was possible to open from May to September every day except Mondays by the inspired introduction of voluntary caretakers, who agreed to live in a caravan nearby for a two week 'holiday' of a unique kind. The many different caretakers have each made their individual contribution to the welcoming atmosphere of the coffee shop and from all reports they have had the refreshing experience of Mosedale itself and of making contact with the interesting visitors who come there. The coffee shop specialises in home made bread, scones and cakes served on locally made pottery; the original benches and tables are still used, as the photographs show.

Some of the wider aims of the original proposal for the use of the meeting house, as for example an outlet for the sale of goods made by the handicapped, have still to be realised, but paintings and drawings made in or near Mosedale are sometimes available; books and pamphlets are also on sale, although these are perhaps of special interest to Quakers and to children. In the minister's gallery there is a small museum of local Quaker interest which still hopefully awaits additions. Many of the Friends mentioned earlier in this book have left their mark in the museum and also in the powerful atmosphere of peace and strength which characterises the place.

The meeting house, to meet the requirements of the national park, is not widely advertised and the outside notice boards have been kept discreet. Nevertheless, it has been appreciated by many visitors, both fell walkers and those exploring the area by car, and much interest has been shown in its origin and history and in the Religious Society of Friends generally. Many people who were previously unaware of the principles and work of the Society now know something of its aims and have a better understanding of what Quakerism stands for in the modern world. Meetings for worship have been greatly strengthened by the presence of Friends staying at the Quaker guest houses at Grasmere and Greystoke and also by members from distant meetings who make the long worthwhile journey to this historic meeting place on the fringe of the birthplace of Quakerism.

There are now no Quakers left in Mosedale, but the influence of Quakerism in this remote and beautiful corner of Cumbria lives on. Meetings for worship are held frequently on Sundays during the summer and the atmosphere of three hundred years of the quiet worship of God in this unique setting has been carefully preserved. No one who visits the meeting house can fail to be moved by the experience, or to respond to its air of simple tranquillity, or to go on their way refreshed by its age old, enduring serenity.

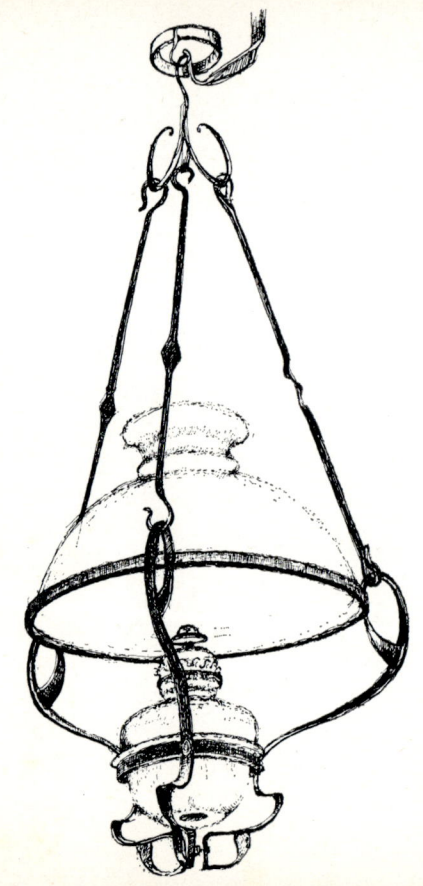

Hand made paraffin
lamp found in the
Meeting House, Mosedale.

24